MYRTLE, RUE AND CYPRESS

Stanislaus Eric Stenbock (1860–1895), Count of Bogesund, was born in the South West England to Lucy Sophia Frerichs, an English cotton heiress, and Count Erich Stenbock, who was of a distinguished Swedish family of the Baltic German House of nobility in Reval. He inherited his family's estates in 1885 and returned to live in his manor house at Kolkbriefly for a period before returning to England. In his life he published three volumes of poetry, *Love, Sleep & Dreams*, *Myrtle, Rue and Cypress*, and *The Shadow of Death*, as well as one collection of short stories, *Studies of Death*. He died as a result of alcoholism and opium addiction.

ERIC, COUNT STENBOCK

MYRTLE, RUE AND CYPRESS

A BOOK OF
Poems, Songs and Sonnets

THIS IS A SNUGGLY BOOK

This edition Copyright © 2019
by Snuggly Books.
All rights reserved.

ISBN: 978-1-943813-94-0

This Snuggly Books edition is an unabridged, slightly amended version of that which was published by Hatchards, in 1883.

In this Book I Dedicate

THE MYRTLE THEREOF
TO SIMEON SOLOMON

THE RUE THEREOF
TO ARVID STENBOCK

AND THE CYPRESS THEREOF TO
THE MEMORY OF
CHARLES BERTRAM FOWLER

CONTENTS

Song I / *11*
Song II / *12*
Song III / *13*
Memoria / *15*
Sonnet I / *17*
Koito and Aemmerik / *18*
Song IV / *20*
Valse des Bacchantes / *21*
Drinking Song / *23*
The Nightingale / *25*
Song V / *27*
A Dream / *28*
The Sea-Gull / *30*
The Song of Love / *31*
The Æolian Harp / *34*
The White Rose / *36*
On a Melody by A. Rubinstein / *38*
Song VI / *39*

A Song of Spring and Autumn / *40*
Sonnet II / *42*
Song VII / *43*
Sonnet III / *45*
Sonnet IV / *46*
Sonnet V / *47*
Golden Dreams / *48*
Song VIII / *50*
Song IX / *51*
The Lunatic Lover / *53*
Sonnet VI / *56*
Sonnet VII / *58*
The Storm / *59*
Song X / *61*
Sonnet VIII / *62*
Reconciliation / *63*
Song XI / *65*
Insomnia / *66*
The Vampyre / *68*
The Singing Sisters / *70*
Sonnet IX / *73*
Song XII / *74*
Song XIII / *75*
Eternal Silence / *76*
Sonnet X / *78*
Sonnet XI / *79*
Sonnet XII / *80*
Sonnet XIII / *81*

MYRTLE,
RUE AND CYPRESS

SONG I.

Preludium.

I DECKED mine altar with faded flowers,
    Because I was sad at heart, you see,
And cared no more, what the passing hours
    In going and coming might bring to me—
I said, "Alas, for the lingering hours
    Shall not bring ought of delight to me."

And yet I sighed for the faded flowers,
    Because my flowers were dead, you see,
Sighed for the flowers and the passing hours
    Because I was sick unto death, you see—
Sick unto death of the desolate hours
    Which came and went so wearily—
And then I looked on my faded flowers
    And sat down and wept for memory.

SONG II.

THEY have long ceased to weep, dear,
    The fleeting hours that fled,
They have cried themselves to sleep, dear—
    Are they asleep or dead?

Is then their sleep so deep, dear,
    They may not wake again—
What—shall we laugh or weep, dear,
    Remembering all our pain?

Love, is thine heart so hardened
    When one tear from thine eyes
Might pour on sin unpardoned
    A rainbow from Paradise?

SONG III.

*"Then Death bethought him of his beautiful garden
where the red and white roses bloom."*
—HANS ANDERSEN.

I HAVE longed for thy beautiful garden,
    The mansion of twilight rooms,
The region of placid faces,
    And flowers, that grow from tombs.

I have longed for thy beautiful garden,
    With the longing of great desire—
Who have walked in barren places,
    Till my feet are shod with fire.

I have longed for thy beautiful garden,
    Whose raiment is woven with sighs,

And a veil of great lamentation
    Is shed as a mist on thine eyes.

I have longed for thy beautiful garden,
    And thy nuptial winding-sheet,
For thy face, ah! tender lover,
    Is gentle and wellnigh sweet.

MEMORIA.

HER name is written in the snow,
In the skies above, in the seas below,
On the cold grey sand that all may know
    Her name is even Memory.
She looks with introverted eyes
On the ravening sea and the riven skies,
And the voice of the shell in her hand replies
    With the old-world stories of the sea.

She hearkeneth to the wild sea's roar,
To the splashing spray on the sad sea-shore,
Pondering on all things gone before,
    Listening unto the lyre of love
Who sings the songs of the old dead days
Of the form once fair and the once loved face,
And the song resounds from the barren ways
    Of the echoing rocks above.

Soul-rending sorrow and piercing pain,
The sickle hath passed through the golden grain—
And wilt thou strive to look yet again
    On the old shed smiles and the old wept tears?
Sheeted shadows of the past,
Seen through the mist veil, pale, aghast
With the white light on their faces cast
    Of the snows of bygone years.

SONNET I.

Composed in St. Isaac's Cathedral, St. Petersburg.

ON waves of music borne it seems to float
    So tender sweet, so fraught with inner pain,
    And far too exquisite to hear again
Above the quivering chords that single note,—
The tremulous fires of the lamp-light gloat
    On the exceeding sweetness of that strain—
    Thou mightest spend a lifetime all in vain
In striving to recall it, yet recall it not.

Therein are mingled mercy, pity, peace,
    Tears wiped away and sorrow comforted,
    Bearing sweet solace and a short relief
    To those, that are acquainted well with grief,
    Reviving for a time joys long since dead,
And granting to the fettered soul release.

KOITO AND AEMMERIK, OR THE LOVES OF THE SUNRISE AND THE SUNSET.

ESTHONIAN LEGEND.

LOVE, love, I have sought thee, sorrowing,
    Through the shuddering hours of the holy night-time,
I inquired of the silver-footed moonbeams
Silently treading on the passionate sea-waves,
And of the bright-eyed watchers at the gate of heaven;
—And seeking thee I could not find thee,
And my tears fell on the green grass and the variegated flowers.

Love, love, I have sought thee, sorrowing,

Through the weary hours of the desolate day-time,
I inquired of the golden smiling sunbeams,
Of the wild winds and the ravening rains,
And of the shadowy fair-faced spirit of the snow;
—And seeking thee I could not find thee,
And my tears fell on the green grass and the
                                    variegated flowers.

Alas, alas! we shall again be rent in sunder,
And the late found joy shall be taken from us;
See, the flame of Love illumines the heavens,
One kiss and one embrace a little lingering.
Let our commingled tears fall on the green grass
   And the variegated flowers.

Note. —Although every work of art should explain itself, we fear we must add here one word of explanation—the legend, namely, on which this poem is founded arises from the fact that in Esthonia on one day in the year (viz. 24 June) the sunrise and sunset take place at the same time.

—S.E.S.

SONG IV.

AND so I stand alone
    And hear the wild waves moan,
Half litten with the melancholy wan star-light;
    I go not any way,
    For all ways wind astray,
And far around falls the unfathomable night.

    Oh you are so unkind—
    And I am grown so blind
That I can scarcely see the pale sad stars above,
    And all in vain I crave,
    Crave what you never gave,
A little light, a little life, a little love.

VALSE DES BACCHANTES.

WITH tremulous feet advancing,
    That hardly touch the ground,
Fair forms embracing, dancing,
    And lightly whirling round,
With the sounds of joy and gladness,
    As a cloud that the moonlight sears
Is mingled a tone of sadness
    From a far-off region of tears.

They tread the mystic measure
    In garments of beauty clad,
Yet even in their pleasure
    There is something passing sad;
None knows what woes come after,
    And none can say where he steers,
And the echo of their laughter
    Is wet with the dew of tears.

Ah, look upon their faces,
    Seen passion-pale through the glare,
Their close and wild embraces,
    Hot lips and flaming hair—
One would say some bitter madness
    Were shed on their tender years,
Unsoftened into sadness
    At the welcome well-spring of tears.

Deliriously turning
    As a flame in the fretful fire,
With the blood in their faces burning
    With the greatness of their desire—
Who knows what woes come after,
    In a twilight of hopes and fears?
"For the roots of the tree of laughter
    Are close to the well of tears."

DRINKING SONG.

DRINK of this wine, my dear,
    The joys of youth are sweet;
Stretch forth thine hand, nor fear
    Of its glowing fruits to eat.

Soon age shall cast its blight
On youth and youth's delight;
Let us enjoy tonight,
    The years are over fleet.

And, darling, let thy voice
Sing thy sweet songs again,
That my spirit may rejoice
    Before the time of pain.

Till age come, withering, scorning,
With withered wreaths adorning

The bitter house of mourning,
    And make thy singing vain.

And kiss me once, my love,
    With thy mouth of wine and fire,
Low murmuring, like the dove,
    And fill thine heart's desire.

Ere age thy soft skin hardens,
Blind age, that no fault pardons,
Cold age, whose withered gardens
    Are hedged with thorn and briar.

THE NIGHTINGALE.

A NIGHTINGALE sat at my window casement,
    And sang and sang to me all night long,
And my soul soared over mine heart's abasement,
    And swam through the night on the waves of
                              song—
By the wings of music my spirit aided
    Flew forth and pierced thro' the heart of the
                              night,
Till sunlight, moonlight, and starlight faded
    In the mystical glow of a purer light.

What passion of music that moves to madness,
    What secret thing doth thy song express,
What excess of joy, that is wellnigh sadness,
    What agony bitter beyond redress?—
What lights of love and what pangs of passion

Through the thrilling throbs of thy wild notes
                                        well,
What words too wondrous for tongue to fashion
    Would suit to thy sweet song, tell, ah tell!

Yet then methought that I caught some meaning,
    Some half suggestion too strange to say,
Some single sheaf, that fell from the gleaning
    Of a heavenly harvest far away—
And my soul was loosed from the bonds that
                                        bound me,
    And my heart for a moment forgot its pain;
But daylight hath woven a shadow around me,
    And the veil half lifted has fallen again.

SONG V.

TO AN AIR OF E. MASSENET.

YEA even though the spring return, my love,
   I can but sigh a little wearily,
     When fair and bright
The flowering fields with blossoms burn, my love,
   Because I know that thou art gone from me,
     And all delight.

And when the last left leaves fall drearily,
   And melancholy mists rise from the rain
     On the dank grass,
I shall still sigh a little wearily,
   Knowing my love shall not come back again,
     Alas, alas!

A DREAM.

THE rain fell fast, the wind was wild,
I saw the image of my child
As in a vision of the night,
At the first grey streak of the morning light.

"Thy face is somewhat pale," I said,
"And thine hair is tangled about thine head;"
"The wind is wild; no wonder then
My hair is tangled," he said again.

"But from thine head unto thy feet
Thy form is wrapped in a long white sheet;"
"My clothes were wet through with the rain,
I put on this sheet till they dry again."

"Come hither, darling, and I will fold
Thee to mine heart, for thy hands are cold;"
"No wonder my hands are cold," he said,
"For very cold are the hands of the *dead*."

THE SEA-GULL.

Ah whither sailing?
    Far over the sea,
So wildly wailing,
As in agony,
Oh sea-gull, slowly swooping, westwardly, wearily!

    Whither, ah, whither,
    Tends thy far floating flight?
    Thither, thither,
    Where at fall of night,
The waves gleam glorious, and golden with rolling
                        and refluent light.

    For there, even there,
    Have I builded my nest,
    In the bright islands, where
    In the waning west
I seek ere the fall of the sunset, at length to lay
                            me to rest.

THE SONG OF LOVE.

(TO A MELODY OF ADOLF HENSELT.)

*"Multae aquae non potuerunt
extinguere charitatem."*

LOVE is enough, though the days be all
                    declining,
  And the world be worn out on her weary,
                    weary way,
Though we sit in the shadow of death in vain
                    repining
    Till the breaking of the day.

We tire of speech, of thought, and frequent
                    moving,
  Our memories are embittered with the
                    shatterings of faith;

Love conquers all we can never tire of loving,
    For love is as strong as Death.

—Love long ago in the far-off silent years
    Sprang forth from the chaos of things,
And there fell a bright light and a gentle dew of
                                tears
    From his eyes, and the winnowing of his wings.

A dew-fall of tears of sweetness, not of sadness,
    From the darkness of night sprang the radiance
                                of day;
The stars in their courses sang forth a hymn of
                                gladness,
    And the shadows fled away.

Through the low fogs of earth 'tis but in fitful
                                gleams
    That His halo can shed forth His rays;
Thro' the lifted veil of sleep and the nebulous
                                woof of dreams
    We alone can behold His face—

Ye have wounded His Heart, ye have mocked Him,
                                ye have bound Him
With wings torn and shattered, to a barren
                                leafless tree,

But the waters could not quench Him, and the
        flood streams have not drowned Him,
    Nor the waves of the bitterer sea.

THE ÆOLIAN HARP.

> *"Wail for the world's wrongs."*
> —SHELLEY.

Thou art the wind's lyre
    That the wind plays upon
  With vibrating tone,
Like the flickering of fire,—
  With wild wailing moan,
Wild as the heart's desire.

I love thy sad song
    And that vibrating tone,
    That is most like a moan,
That the winds bear along,
    As they shudder and groan
And wail for the world's wrong.

Light breezes, that blow;
    That bear with you along
    The soft current of song
With sound sweet and low,
    Wail for the world's wrongs
And weep for the world's woe.

Ah, languishing lyre,
    With rhythmical flow
    Of sound sweet and low
Like the flickering of fire,
    Weep for the world's woe,
Wail for the heart's desire.

THE WHITE ROSE.

It is so sad because it is so sweet, you see,
    The white rose is so pale, almost too pale,
  So light and slight, fleetingly fair and frail,
  That one would surely say its sweet shall fail
When the wild withering winds shall rive it
                             ruthlessly—
So we must needs weep hearing that moving
                                 melody.

It is so sweet, because it is so sad, you see,
    As the grey grave-stone, where the green grass
                                 grows,
  Or the sad seashore where the full flood flows,
  Or the winds withering the wild white rose,
With every painful petal dropping droopingly,—
Why doth the white rose wreath itself around
                                 that melody?

All sweet things have some sad in them, you see,
    And all sad things some sweet, and this is so
    Because Love liveth in a world of woe
    Made miserable by his most mighty foe,
Who dwells in the dark depths, laughing
                                   exultingly—
And this is the mad meaning of that moving
                                       melody.

ON A MELODY BY A. RUBINSTEIN.

IT yearns, and burns, and turns,
    And yearns and turns again
With the measure of the pleasure
    Of the slain vain strain of pain—

    And wanders weirdly on,
      Till it touches at that tone
Which wrings the last drop from the height of all
        delight,
    And the heart's dull ache it slakes,
    Till the heart for love's sake breaks,
In one wild instant, when the world sinks out of
        sight.

SONG VI.

"Vulnerasti cor meum."

AS the wings of a dove on a hard stone wall
    Are torn, and shattered and frayed,
As the relics of spring at the first frost fall,
    When stricken, wither and fade;

So the wings of Love and the heart of Love
    Are wounded and pierced and torn,
And shattered and frayed as the wings of a dove,
    By the cold world's bitter scorn.

A SONG OF SPRING AND AUTUMN.

"Vox turturis audita est in terra nostra."

ARISE, my belovèd,
The winter is past,
The might of the snow-storm,
The rage of the blast.
The leaves of the myrtle
By light wings are fanned,
And the voice of the turtle
Is heard in our land.

Arise, my belovèd,
Come let us go
To our beautiful garden,
Where sweet spices flow—
To gather the roses,

And fruit of the vine,
Where the wild fawn reposes,
My vineyard is mine.

Lie down, my belovèd,
The swallows are flown,
And the songs of the spring-time
Are over and gone.
The stars of the myrtle
Are fallen away,
And the voice of the turtle
Is heard not all day.

Lie down, my belovèd,
The vine-fruit is shed,
And our beautiful garden
Is withered and dead.
All torn are the roses
With the wild ravening rains;
When the wearied eye closes
Love only remains.

SONNET II.

"Osculet me osculis oris sui."

AH, kiss me with the kisses of thy mouth,
    Thy love is sweeter to my heart than wine,
Sweeter than sleep from some strange anodyne,
Sweeter than spices, gathered in the South,
Or hidden well-water in time of drouth;
    And let thine arms about mine head entwine,
    Mine own beloved, seeing thou art mine,
And kiss me with the kisses of thy mouth.

Ah sweet, mine heart is ravished utterly
    By thy fair body fashioned without fleck,
By one long look that glimmereth from thine eye,
    By one long look that leaneth down thy neck.
Kiss me with kisses, love, I faint, I pine,
Thy love is sweeter to mine heart than wine.

SONG VII.

UNTIL the daylight breaketh
    And the shadows flee away,
I sleep, mine heart yet waketh,
    I heard thy voice as I lay.

At the time when the night was waning,
    And the light of the stars grew pale,
I heard thy sad complaining,
    Thy soft and dovelike wail.

'Tis the voice of my belovèd
    Who calleth unto me;
Shall not my heart be movèd,
    Shall I not ope to thee?

Love, guide me to the mountain
    Of frankincense and myrrh,

To the sweet and silver fountain
    That my footsteps may not err!

Stir not my love till he waketh,
    I charge thee, my love, to stay
Until the daylight breaketh
    And the shadows flee away.

SONNET III.

ON THE NEMEWESKI WATERFALL.

OH rapid, rushing, rhythmically rippling river,
    And crash of mighty waters wonderful,
So terrible, and yet withal so beautiful,
That one were wellnigh fain to while for ever
Watching the silver-footed moonbeams quiver
    With silent tread, and movement mystical,
    Hearing the cadence of the waterfall,
Feeling the calm night air with ecstasy shiver.

An holy hymn unspeakably sublime,
    Sung by a god unto some greater god,
The greeting of eternity and time
    Wells up from every rhythmic period
Of that flood's singing, like to the world's tears
Responding to the music of the spheres.

SONNET IV.

METHOUGHT I heard the music of the spheres,
   A sound of awful music ringing loud
   From each pulsation of the heart of God,
Along the ways of many thousand years,
And through the night a falling as of tears,
   Of bitter tears of blood, that cried aloud
   For mercy and for justice unto God,
Who turned from their strong crying his deaf ears.

A flood of tears of blood the night sky sears
   The bitterness of congregated woe,
The gathered lamentation of long years,
The tears of Love; who mid a world of tears
   Lives overcome by his most mighty foe,
Who ruleth the revolving of the spheres.

SONNET V.

ON A DREAM.

COVER thy face, for there are fearful things
    That flicker through the visions of the night,
    Causing the soul to shiver with affright,
The dreadful images the Dream-god brings;—
I saw a dark form flying without wings,
Through falling darkness severed with strange light,
    Fleeing away in wild and fearful flight,
And yet for ever running round in rings.

And as I wondered why that form fled so,
    I saw another form with visage dread
    Following fast upon the form that fled,
A dagger in his hand, a bitter foe—
Alas, my love, the flying form was thine,
The face of the pursuer, that was mine!

GOLDEN DREAMS.

AH gloom devoid of gladness! ah the sadness!
ah the madness!
Ah vision-rending dusk, dream-scorning
morning light!—
Ye have woken, ye have broken that fleeting dream
of gladness,
They are vanished, they are banished, the sweet
visions of the night.

I dreamed of you, my darling, that I again had
found you
(I had dreamed it twice already, so I knew it
was not true)—
That I again had found you, and wound mine
arms around you,
And your eyes looked up so sweetly, just as
they used to do.

And you told me that you loved me, and you said
                              that you had missed me,
   And that we, though rent in sunder, should be
                              brought together again,
And so warmly you embraced me, and so tenderly
                              you kissed me,
   That my heart was glad within me as the
                              sunshine after rain.

And you told me, ah so sweetly, you would stay
                              with me for ever,
   And I had so much to tell you that I scarce
                              knew what to say,
When a single streak of sunlight this golden dream
                              did sever,
   And the fabric of the vision like a vapour rolled
                              away.

Is so very little pleasure worth such bitter
                              disappointment,
   And is a joy so fleeting worth so long an after
                              pain?
Are the wounds, that were so galling, cured by
                              the costly ointment?—
   For I knew, dear, 'twas not true, dear, that you
                              would come back again.

SONG VIII.

(COMPOSED IN A DREAM.)

THERE shall be no more crying
    But mute eternal grief,
Beyond all sound of sighing,
    Because beyond relief.

Thy tears are all collected
    In a deep clear crystal well,
Thy passions are all planted
    In meadows of asphodel.

There shall be no more crying,
    No change of night and day,
No sound of sobbing or sighing,
    For the old things are passed away.

SONG IX.

<blockquote>

AH play to me
    That melody
For I am sick of love.
    I think all day
    Of one far away
Whom that tune reminds me of.

    Day is as night,
    Without the light
That flows from his love-lit eyes.
    Night waste as day
    I pine away,
My spirit within me dies.

    I cannot sleep,
    I only weep,

</blockquote>

Bereft of his soft embrace;
        And through the day
        I think alway
On that sweet familiar face.

THE LUNATIC LOVER.

AH, love, I dreamed of thee last night,
    Of strange lips kissing me,
With subtle penetrating pain—
    A moon veil shrouded thee
(I shudder, when I think of this,
    That a moon veil shrouded thee);
Thine eyes had in them all the light
    Of the moonlight on the sea.

Thine eyes are beautiful and soft,
    As the eyes of Seraphim,—
Ah, limpid liquid lustrous eyes,
    Sad eyes half bright, half dim,
Half without light, half brighter bright,
    Than the eyes of Seraphim.

That strange magnetic glance, that gleams
    From those mystic eyes of vair,
That face so brilliantly pale,
    And yet withal so fair,—
Love-pale and passion-pale, and yet,
    So marvellously fair,—
That countenance corpse-like refined,
    And subtle coloured hair.

Thy slender limbs that seem to burn
    Thy vesture through with fire,
That serpentine electric form
    Half quivering with desire,
Thy movements full of grace divine
    As the music of the lyre—
(Alas! for whoso looks on thee
    Feels new and strange desire,
The serpent winds around his heart,
    His soul is turned to fire,
As though within his veins there ran
    A current of Hell fire.)

I know, I know that long ago
    The moon with silver feet
Crept to thy bed, close to thine head,
    And kissed thy forehead, sweet,
Giving thy lips strange wine to drink,

  And alien flesh to eat,
And apples culled from the Dead Sea,
  Which are the serpent's meat,
Fruit from the tree by the Dead Sea
  Whose fruit is death to eat.

Note. —We have deemed it more judicious to represent the rest of this poem by ********.
—S.E.S.

SONNET VI.

(ON THE FIRST MOVEMENT OF BEETHOVEN'S 'MOONLIGHT SONATA'.)

IN a strange land full of strange creeping things
    West of the waning sunset—where?—
                      who knows?
    A silent shadow-land, whence no wind blows,—
There sits a solitary bird and sings
A mournful melody, and waves his wings,
    Unto a solitary rose, that grows
    By a strange solitary stream, that flows
With mystical melodious murmurings.

And much I marvelled in that lonesome land,
    To hear that strange bird's solitary song;
    So I stood silently and listened long

By a wind not of this world faintly fanned—
And the song pained me with a wild delight,
The rose looked white bathed in the weird
                                          moonlight.

SONNET VII.

SOME strange and thrilling chord struck carelessly
   Long lingering on lute or viol string,
   Snatches from songs thy voice was wont to sing,
Stray strains of wild and wandering melody
Ring from the soul its utmost agony;
   Such tear-laden remembrances they bring
   Of thee whose foot-fall was as lute-playing,
Whose face was even as melody to me.

Though like leaves autumn-scattered from the trees
   Thy life be shed, thy spirit did not die,
But liveth alway in the sound of these;
   That chord was as the glancing of thine eye!
And as I touched that tone I felt thy face
Looking on me with weary wistful gaze.

THE STORM.

LOVE, hold me fast,
    Hold closely and bind me.
In thine arms closely wind me,
    That Death may find us together at last.

    Ah God, ah God!
Wilt thou now smite us,
'Twill but delight us,
    Thy scorpions are milder than a rod.

    We count it bliss,
For, love, what bliss is
More sweet than thy kiss is,
    And even God hath not robbed me of this.

    Let tempests rave
Beyond all morrow,

All joy, all sorrow,
>   We lie entwined in our deep sea grave.

>   I, love, with thee
Will lie together
All wind and weather
>   Where the waves hardly waver, or storms
>>   shake the sea.

SONG X.

TO A RUSSIAN AIR.

AH sweet, those eyes, that used to be so tender,
    Are grown so cold, as bitter cold as death;
The burnt-out ashes fall into the fender,
    None shall revive the flame that perisheth.

So leave me, love, just kiss me once, then turning,
    Go forth from me before the fall of day;
'Twere better, love, to leave the ashes burning
    Than wait too late till they are burnt away.

SONNET VIII.

SOFTLY and swiftly falling flakes of snow
    Cover and kiss the fallen autumn leaves,
Where the wild wind is as a voice, that grieves,
Wearily, wildly, wailing words of woe.
Cover me with thy kisses like the snow,
    Burying bitter memories like dead leaves,
    Within mine heart, where a sad voice yet
                                  grieves
For a lost lingering love, lost long ago.

Softly and swiftly let thy kisses rain,
    Completely covering me with all delight,
And as the snow-fall over hill and plain,
    Clothe me with fair apparel pure and white.
Then is the old wound wholly healed again,
    The barren field made beautiful and bright.

RECONCILIATION.

DARLING, what shall we say
    Today of yesterday?
Those things are passed away,
Alas!—shall nothing stay?—
Shall a year's love be as waste day's play?

    Yet surely it were vain,
    To strive to revive again
    The old love, the old pain;
    Let all slain things lie slain
In the short spell of sunshine after rain.

    And let no flame aspire,
    From the ashes of desire,
    And flare with flickering fire
    Upon Love's funeral pyre;
Let no sad wind wail chords on the riven lyre.

So, darling, let us say,
It were the better way,
To leave last year's decay,
The fallen flowers of May,
Let the snow cover all with white array.

SONG XI.

ENTWINE thy limbs around me, love, and let
    Thy sweet soft face lean closer kissing me,
Ah sweet! thy beauty stings and burns me, yet
    Alas, my love, my heart is far from thee!

Cast forth upon the waves and rent in twain,
    A riven relic, severed of the sea,
I fear 't will hardly learn to love again,—
    Alas, my love, my heart is far from thee.

Sweet, be not angered with me, kiss me yet,
    And throw thine arms around me lovingly—
Thou art so beautiful, shall I forget?
    Alas, my love, my heart is far from thee.

INSOMNIA.

A SERPENT is bound about her head,
Her eyes are closed, but she is not dead;
She is not dead, and she doth not sleep,
Too weary to wake and too worn to weep
Although her agony is deep,
She hath not wherewithal to slake
The pressing pain of her eyes, that ache,
Her mouth is writhen with the pain
Of one that shall not smile again.

O thou, whose life is thy delight,
Whose eyes are brilliantly bright,
Who sleepest sweetly every night,
With the light of youth upon thee shed
As an aureole round thy glad head
With benedictions garlanded;
Whose feet flash flame and whose lips drop myrrh;
Wilt thou turn from thy way to pity her?

If thou shouldst touch her tired eyes
Perchance she would soften her stifled sighs,
And thine healing hand work a miracle,
And a torrent of tears from her worn eyes well,
And in the glad stream her sad soul should steep,
And the touch of thy lips should send her sleep.

THE VAMPYRE.

*"Ich lieb' dich, mich reizt deine schöne Gestalt
Und bist du nicht willig so brauch' ich Gewalt."*

I WOULD seek thee in secret places
   In the darkest hour of night,
Embrace thee with serpent embraces,
   Delight thee with strange delight.

In a serpent's coils entwine
   Thy supple and exquisite form,
And drink from thy veins like wine
   Thy blood delicious and warm.

With slow soft sensual sips
   Draw the life from the tender spray,
And brush from thy soft lithe lips
   The bloom of thy boyhood away.

I would breathe with the breath of thy mouth
    And pang thee with perfect pain;
And the vital flame of thy youth
    Should live in my limbs again.

Till thy vital elastical form
    Should gradually fade and fail,
And thy blood in my veins flow warm,
    And glow in my face, that was pale.

THE SINGING SISTERS.

OH the three singing sisters, they sat and span,
While the red thread through their faint
                    fingers rightly ran.

Oh their faces were fearful, their forms were tall,
Their garments fell like a funeral pall,
And they sang a song as they span their thread,
And they that dwelt among the dead
Came and sat at the feet of those sisters three,
And heard their soul-thrilling threnody.
Some sat and listened, some stood aloof
Watching them weaving their weird woof.

And the three singing sisters sat and span,
And the red thread through their faint fingers
                          rightly ran.

And this was the song that those sisters sung,
"Go take thy lot the wide world among,
And on thy forehead I write my curse
From thy cradle unto thine hearse;
Be miserable among happiness,
Be filled with good things in thy distress
Visible for thine eyes shall be
Such shameful sights, as none may see;
Such sounds thine ears shall hear,
As shall cause thy soul to quake with fear;
My bitter draught thy tongue shall taste
And drain the dregs to the very last,
Thy soul shall seek and thine heart shall crave
Such things, as thou mayest not have;
If thou love any among men,
Then shall the living all be slain,
But the dead shall rise again,
Rise again with a purple stain
That all may know them to be such
As have felt the contagion of thy touch."

And the three singing sisters sat and span,
And the red thread through their faint fingers
                                        rightly ran.

And then methought in that same place,
In the depths of the darkness, a fearfuller face

    Laughed with a mad malignity,
    And laughed and laughed eternally

While the three singing sisters sat and span,
And the red thread through their faint fingers
                                      rightly ran.

SONNET IX.

VISIT me sometimes in the dreams of night,
    Until the daybreak and the shadows flee
  Away, and let my soul commune with thee;
Grant me at least this brief and cold delight—
Canst thou not cross the veil—ah, that I might
    Lie but one night in dreams embracing thee,
    And feel thee near me, hear thy voice, and see
Thy face once more, and gladden in the sight.

My love is dead, and comes not back again,
    Yet once in the still watches of one night
    I felt the silence cleft with a low moan
From a loved voice, that sighed as if in pain,
    A spirit's lips were pressed upon mine own,
    —Then I arose to curse the wan daylight.

SONG XII.

THEY told me my love had left me,
    So I wept, and wept, and wept,
Till I could weep no longer,
    Then I laid me down and slept.

But my true love had not left me,
    And stood by my grave in pain,
And his tears fell softly on me,
    But I shall not wake again.

And this is the story, darling,
    That I read in the depths of thine eyes,
Those eyes that are yet as virgin
    To tears, as thy lips to sighs.

SONG XIII.

TO A BOY.

'TIS even a delight, dear,
   To gaze upon thy face,
To love the life within thee,
   Fair fashioned, full of grace.
But in the ark of thy body
   The soul hath no resting-place.

And so there is that about thee
   Which left me not content,
As the sighing strings of the wind-harp,
   Where the wind's weird wailings went,
Or the poor pressed petals that still keep
   A thought of the rose's scent.

ETERNAL SILENCE.

STRIVE not to lift the veil,
Lest lifting it thou die, but lightly look
Upon the open pages of the book,
But do not try to read therein the tale,
Lest thine heart utterly should faint and fail.

And do not pause to think
Upon that mystery of misery;
Look down into the depths of the deep sea,
But do not linger long upon the brink,
Lest fascinated, thou fall therein and sink.

For silence holds a rose I?
Eternally upon his lips, lest he,
Whose eyes have looked upon the mystery
Should tell to others of the things he knows,
And fill the woe-worn world with woefuller woes.

SONNET X.

THE SLEEPING WATERS.

I STOOD in a strange city in a dream,
   Luridly lighted, lifeless, lorn and lone,
  Horror without moan or groan, frozen into stone.
Mid this weird woe there did not flow a stream,
Nor fast, nor slow, it did not flow, that stream,
   Its drear dark dismal depths told forth no tone,
   And in the stately streets on grey-grown stone
Was writ in characters of silver gleam:

"The sleeping waters—ah, they are deadly chill,
And strangely still, and who is there that will
Wade through the waveless waters wide and deep,
Which do not weep, but sleep, and sleep, and sleep?"
The sleeping waters—ah! I stood upon the brink,
And my soul shivering seemed to shrink and sink.

SONNET XI.

IT might have been, but ah, it was too late—
   Doomed to be disappointed—and how long
  Shall I sit and sing that soul-sick song
Of which my soul is sadly satiate?
Which curious counterchange of fitful fate
   Led thee to me, for whom I had longed so long,
   Of many days and hours, choosing the wrong,
Even that heart-sick hour called "too late"?

And thine eyes looked on me so piteously,
   Beautiful eyes, that thrilled and filled with tears,
  Tears, even for one of which I had yearned for
                                  years,
And thine hand lingered a little lovingly;—
Even for this little, love, long did I wait,
And when it came it was too late—too late.

SONNET XII.

ALL of no use, 'twas all of no avail,
    I lived my life, I loved my love in vain;
  Yea, of all pains this is the bitterest pain,
In sooth 'twere hard to tell a sadder tale.
The long hours come and go, and weep and wail,
    All wound thee, and the last shall leave thee slain,
  The joy missed once shall not come back again,
And all thy tears shall be of no avail.

Is thy youth fled,—and are thy dreams all dead?
    Is thy one flower trodden under foot
In bye-ways, where the way-worn wanderers tread,
    Or hath it bloomed and perished without fruit?
Or is the fruit thereof all plucked and shed?
    Or hath thine own hand killed it at the root?

SONNET XIII.

"Om mani padme hum."

AH, the jewel is in the lotus, and one rose
    Blooms, though all fainter flowers fade away,
Though all be dark, yet there is somewhere day;
Though all the sea be salt, one pure stream flows,
Though all are full of cursing, one bestows
    A blessing that shall not be torn away.
    There is one way, though all ways wind astray,
One path of peace from fire-footed foes.

Oh living love, from whose wide wounded heart
    Red streams of blood flow through the
                              firmament,
Though all forsake thee, yet will I not depart,
    But in thy worship will I rest content,
Though there be left none else to worship thee,
And all bow down before thine enemy.

A PARTIAL LIST OF SNUGGLY BOOKS

G. ALBERT AURIER *Elsewhere and Other Stories*
S. HENRY BERTHOUD *Misanthropic Tales*
LÉON BLOY *The Tarantulas' Parlor and Other Unkind Tales*
JAMES CHAMPAGNE *Harlem Smoke*
FÉLICIEN CHAMPSAUR *The Latin Orgy*
BRENDAN CONNELL *Clark*
BRENDAN CONNELL *Unofficial History of Pi Wei*
ADOLFO COUVE *When I Think of My Missing Head*
QUENTIN S. CRISP *Graves*
QUENTIN S. CRISP *Rule Dementia!*
LADY DILKE *The Outcast Spirit and Other Stories*
BERIT ELLINGSEN *Now We Can See the Moon*
BERIT ELLINGSEN *Vessel and Solsvart*
EDMOND AND JULES DE GONCOURT *Manette Salomon*
GUIDO GOZZANO *Alcina and Other Stories*
RHYS HUGHES *Cloud Farming in Wales*
J.-K. HUYSMANS *Knapsacks*
COLIN INSOLE *Valerie and Other Stories*
JUSTIN ISIS *Pleasant Tales II*
JUSTIN ISIS (editor) *Marked to Die: A Tribute to Mark Samuels*
VICTOR JOLY *The Unknown Collaborator and Other Legendary Tales*
BERNARD LAZARE *The Mirror of Legends*
BERNARD LAZARE *The Torch-Bearers*
MAURICE LEVEL *The Shadow*
JEAN LORRAIN *Errant Vice*
JEAN LORRAIN *Masks in the Tapestry*
JEAN LORRAIN *Nightmares of an Ether-Drinker*
JEAN LORRAIN *The Soul-Drinker and Other Decadent Fantasies*

ARTHUR MACHEN *N*
ARTHUR MACHEN *Ornaments in Jade*
CAMILLE MAUCLAIR *The Frail Soul and Other Stories*
CATULLE MENDÈS *Bluebirds*
CATULLE MENDÈS *To Read in the Bath*
EPHRAÏM MIKHAËL *Halyartes and Other Poems in Prose*
LUIS DE MIRANDA *Who Killed the Poet?*
OCTAVE MIRBEAU *The Death of Balzac*
CHARLES MORICE *Babels, Balloons and Innocent Eyes*
DAMIAN MURPHY *Daughters of Apostasy*
DAMIAN MURPHY *The Star of Gnosia*
KRISTINE ONG MUSLIM *Butterfly Dream*
YARROW PAISLEY *Mendicant City*
URSULA PFLUG *Down From*
JEAN RICHEPIN *The Bull-Man and the Grasshopper*
DAVID RIX *A Suite in Four Windows*
FREDERICK ROLFE (BARON CORVO)
    An Ossuary of the North Lagoon and Other Stories
JASON ROLFE *An Archive of Human Nonsense*
BRIAN STABLEFORD *Spirits of the Vasty Deep*
BRIAN STABLEFORD (editor)
    Decadence and Symbolism: A Showcase Anthology
COUNT ERIC STENBOCK *Love, Sleep & Dreams*
COUNT ERIC STENBOCK *Studies of Death*
DOUGLAS THOMPSON *The Fallen West*
TOADHOUSE *Gone Fishing with Samy Rosenstock*
JANE DE LA VAUDÈRE *The Demi-Sexes and The Androgynes*
JANE DE LA VAUDÈRE *Syta's Harem and Pharaoh's Lover*
RENÉE VIVIEN *Lilith's Legacy*
RENÉE VIVIEN *A Woman Appeared to Me*

www.ingramcontent.com/pod-product-compliance
Lightning Source LLC
Chambersburg PA
CBHW020129130526
44591CB00032B/577